THE DIRT ROAD

THE DIRT ROAD
Living on the dirt road

SANDRA EATMON

XULON PRESS

Xulon Press
2301 Lucien Way #415
Maitland, FL 32751
407.339.4217
www.xulonpress.com

© 2017 by Sandra Eatmon

All rights reserved solely by the author. The author guarantees all contents are original and do not infringe upon the legal rights of any other person or work. No part of this book may be reproduced in any form without the permission of the author. The views expressed in this book are not necessarily those of the publisher.

Unless otherwise indicated, Scripture quotations taken from the King James Version (KJV) – *public domain.*

Printed in the United States of America.

ISBN-13: 9781545611937

To my children
Ke'sha
Kimberly
Tommy
The dirt road was the worst of time
but when you came along it became
the best of times.

I would like to think my older brother mama man son who gave me his permission to write this book. Thank you, Lawrence, for being understanding and supporting of this book, it has to help me to be liberated from my past.

To my other sibling, I know you may have your version of the dirt road, but I pray that in some way you will find liberty.

Table of Contents

The dirt road 1
The making of the dirt road 3
Coming to stay with mama 7
South Carolina Witches. 13
The babies are coming 15
Juke Joint 17
Her Husband 20
Hospital and mishap 25
Missing school 31
Kindergarten with the boys 33
Still not happy at home. 35
Those little old church ladies 37
That most horrible night 41
Living through pain. 44
Hog killing 48
State Fair 54
Disappointment 59
Traveling Time 64

The Dirt Road

What qualifies a person as an overcomer? Who decides whether or not someone's life experiences defines what it means to be an overcomer?

I can tell you firsthand what qualifies me, to bear the title of an overcomer. It was in my knowing that somehow, someway and someday life would yield unto me something better. I would repeat this affirmation to myself daily. I believed it would not be 'this' way always.

Through many struggles, heartaches and pain, this truth, is what I stood on as a youth. I had nothing else to stand on or believe in. Life was not easy growing up on the dirt road that holds so many memories, good, bad and ugly. Journey

The Dirt Road

with me as I walk down a dirt road in rural North Carolina about a half of a mile to the city line.

The making of the dirt road

On any given day, there were cars traveling down the dirt road. They always had to squeeze past one another, because the narrowness of the road was not wide enough for two lanes. You could hear the laughter of children riding their bikes up and down the dirt road. You saw people walking to the top of the dirt road to catch a ride into town. School buses stopped at the top of the dirt road for school children. On some mornings, there would be fighting amongst kids who did not live on the dirt road. My biggest highlight would be racing to the mailbox after school to get the mail. On the weekend my sister and I would go to the top of the dirt road to count cars as they went by. We would share which car we like the most because that was the kind of car we would own when we became adults. The dirt road was special in its way, and there was never a dull moment. It was so full of life; children played hopscotch, jump rope, jack rocks, and other games in the summer. People walked into each other houses; there were no locked doors. Mama man sister always had the grill fired up. She was deemed a good cook on the grill or in the house. Sometimes they would take turns cooking on the grill because mama man was a good cook as well. He would always give his mama credit for teaching him how to cook at an early age. He professed that she said he needed to know in case he never married or had a woman in his life to take care of him. Mama who was an excellent cook as well.

Most days you would see grandpa sitting on that old porch with chewing tobacco or snuff laid up in the corner of his mouth. He would spit in that old spit can that he kept right by his side. When he thought that he had that old spit can full, you would hear him say to whoever was near him, "take my spit can out by that old tree and empty it!" I would say, "that's nasty" and empty that old spit can anyway. After the spit can was emptied, Grandpa would lean back in his old chair and go to sleep. He would sleep a lot on that old porch. You could always catch him sleeping. They say he had what they called, that sleeping disease. You could always expect to see Grandma sitting on the porch on Saturday evenings. She would study her Sunday school lessons. I would often go and sit with her, and we would talk about whatever she was studying or reading, but mostly, grandma spent her time telling me how nice I was. She would say you are one of your mama's best children. She would always say things to me like, "I declare child the older you get, the better you look. The older you get, the better you had me feeling some kind of," but she always had a cleanup version. She would say, "you know your mama has some good looking children." Sometimes grandma would be studying her note singing book, and sometimes she would just break out singing songs, one of those songs that just didn't make any sense to me, the words would do RAY ME FA SOL LAW TEE DO RAY ME and boy, she would be singing that song as if she had it down to a science.

After our small talks, I would walk back to my home, that old red brick house and hang out under the old car porch. That was our hangout place. We would sit that old record player outside and dance. Other neighborhood children would come and join in, and we would have ourselves a good ole time. The dirt road was filled with life, laughter, and love in its way by a neighborhood of kinfolks. I think the only ones who were not any real kin was a mama and her three three older children that she had before she met her man.

Coming to stay with mama

I remember being three years old when I first felt my mother's love. She had given me a bath and put nice clean clothes on me. It felt special because I had her all to myself. That day, she had taken me to the store and bought me candy. I felt as if heaven had opened up. The sky was a beautiful blue, and I could feel the presence of something good that day.

My brother and I had not been with mama long. She came to Carthage, NC to get us. I was later told that mama's side of the family was big and that mama had lots of aunts. I cannot recall living in Carthage but I do remember having a pair of black patent leather shoes which were hard to put on and even harder to take off. The shoes had so many buckles that my relationship with them was one of love and hate. I hated putting them on, but I loved how they shined. My grandma would acknowledge my struggle and helped me to take them off. I barely remember my mama's mama. She would give us watermelon often, and I remember the flies would always come around when she did. I was later told by a cousin they were poor country people would who voice their opinion in an unyielding way and would fight you at a drop of the hat which would sometimes land someone in jail or even have someone banned from town. There was also a road named in honor of the family because it was so large.

We lived with mama and her new man, who would later become her husband. The story goes mama daddy died while she was still in her mama's belly or maybe she was one year old at the time, I really can't get that part straight. I would say mama was one year old when her daddy drowned. He drowned in the rock quarry. Mama showed me a picture of her and her sister , where he had written on the back of the picture, Ralley's babies, which indicated to me that he died around the time that mama was a year old.

Years later, a year before I was born, mama's mama died of heart. I heard them say she loved to drink, and that she was given poisoned liquor by her then husband. Mama says she spoke with her mama a few days before she died. Mama was planning to move back to NC, but before she could finish packing, she received a call notifying her that her mother had died. She was very sad when she told me that story.

I was a nosey child. I always asked mama a lot of question because I was very interested in the missing puzzle pieces of our family history. My dead grandma had a child by her husband whom she was married to at the time of her death, unfortunately, this child, who was five, saw her mother dead in a chair. This event scarred her and left her with mental challenges. She went to live with her older sister who cared for her until she graduated from high school. We soon lost track of her all together.

Now grandpa, mama daddy's side was from Georgia. I guessed that's why mama had her three oldest children living in different places with different relatives. The Georgia side was kind of well off. They had businesses, stores, rental houses, grocery stores, and dry cleaners. I remember when mama got the phone call from her Aunt in Georgia asking her to come and get a child. Her aunt stated that she could not keep up with her any longer because she runs and hides under the house. Mama's aunt said that she was too old to go under the house to get this child who did not listen or do what she was told to do. Mama, her new man, my younger brother and I went to get the child who I learned was my older sister. I did get to see the place where this child would run and hide under the house. The house was so high up that we could stand up under the house! As we drove back to North Carolina, there was a sense of the family present. Mama had all of her children with her now. It looked as if things were good and remain so as we settled into becoming family.

My older sister started school immediately. This left me and my younger brother at home with mama during the day. I couldn't wait for my older sister to arrive home. I asked mama a lot of questions because I was so excited to get to know my sister. It always felt as if she was gone for a long time. My brother spent a lot of time with mama's man during the day helping to build our house. He was a good little worker, carrying buckets of nails, wood, and water for him. Little children started working early. We too had to earn our keeps as we were shaping into our family lifestyle.

Mama was a beautiful woman; she had a smile that would light up the room. She had many talents and skills. She would make homemade soap because she was thrifty with a dollar and I guess those were hard times. She would make our clothes from scratch, she needed no pattern to go by, she would sew those dresses by hand, and they would look like they were brought right out the store. We would wear our dresses with pride because mama had made them. They were beautiful. I loved showing them off at school. Mama would only make dresses on a special occasion like picture day or when we had to wrap the Maypole at school. It was such a great day to wrap the May Pole, which meant we had no classes, it was a day of festival and fun.

Mama was also a gifted cosmetologist. Mama could fix some hair. She was always called on to fix the young girl's hair in the neighborhood, especially for the first day of school. There was always a line of girls waiting to get their hair done. They would come with money in their hands. Some would have standing two weeks appointments. She would straighten their hair with a hot comb, and it would look like they just got a relaxer. The young girls loved it. They came back every year for a fresh new hair do for the first day of school. Now sometimes after she finish doing everyone else's hair, she would be too tired to fix my sister and my hair. We had to wait because mama was plain old tired.

South Carolina Witches

No long after getting settled into our new family lifestyle, they say mama man had to hide somewhere in South Carolina to see the root doctor, some called them witch doctor. Once a fight broke out, and he either shot or stabbed a man to death. Some say he darn near cut that man neck off. He then ran and hid somewhere in South Carolina for about a week. While there he went to the witch doctor house where they mix him a liquid to drink. Those witch doctors worked their black magic on him so that he could get him off for murder. Well, whatever that witch doctor did must have worked, because he never did a day in jail, he got away scot-free for killing that man. Some say it had something to do with protecting a family member. I think mama loved that old song, stand by your man. Mama stuck by her man wherever he went; she was right by his side.

Now, whenever there was any legal trouble, and it looked as if it was not working in his favor, I am told he would go to see these witches so that they could work their magic. They must have known what to do because after seeing them, things always worked out for him. Mama stuck right by her man side. When he went to court, and his case was dismissed it wasn't long until we were back to our normal way of living.

The babies are coming

My younger brother was five years old at the time mama started having children by her man. I used his age to keep up with the babies they were coming so fast. The first one came, then the second, third and fourth. They were only nine months apart. At the age of six, I could not understand how the babies were coming one right after the other.

In between the children came fussing, cussing and hard living for mama. She works from the sun up to sundown to keep our house in order, to put food on the table, canning food for the winter and she still found time to work part time at the Holiday Inn. Living not only became hard for mama, it soon became hard for her three older children as well.

We started working at a very early age, chopping wood, carrying the wood to the house, drawing water from the well, washing baby diapers outside in the cold with cold water and then having to hang them out to dry in the cold. Our noses would be running and hands were frozen barely able to open the clothes pen. I think mama told her man that we couldn't reach the cloths line, so he lowered it to make sure those clothes got hung up. Helping mama take care of those little boys was not always an easy thing to do. With my sister and me doing all the household chores it was a piece of cake for a little girl.

Juke Joint

Sometime later I was awakened by the call of mama's voice bidding me to come and see something. I must have been seven or eight at the time. I got up from my daytime nap; it must have been three or four in the evening. I went into the kitchen and saw mama standing at the back looking through the screen door. I rubbed my eyes, unsure of what I was looking at, and mama pointed and said that the old juke joint was on fire. I had never seen such a fire; the whole place was burnt down to the ground. I started to cry as mama, and I stood there watching it burn. It looked like a towering inferno. Mama says, Sandra why are you crying? That old juke joint held some special memories. The grown folks would often go there on the weekend to dance, party, drink and have what they called, a good ole time. Young children were not permitted to go there, only during the week when it served as a community story. Even then mama wasn't big on us going. Once mama needed a bag of sugar from the store, and she called for me to get it. The old man that ran the store stayed in the back of the store. As I entered in, I hollered to the old man, because he could not get around like he used to. "Mama need a bag of sugar!" I yelled. He said, "ok go ahead and get what you need and leave the money on the counter." A few day later I thought I would sneak to the store without mama knowing, I say to the old man, "I a need to get a piece candy!" He said, "ok get what you need," just as he did before and "leave your money on the counter," only this time, I did not have money to leave on the counter. I took the candy and left the store. The problem came as I could not enjoy the candy because I felt really bad knowing that I had taken candy without paying for it and Lord, please don't let mama find out because that surely would be a butt whipping. Praise be to God, mama never found out, and I never took another piece of candy without paying for it. Mama say, Sandra, why are you crying? I said, it's scary did the old man burn up too? They did say the old man made it out alive and stayed with some family member until his death.

Her Husband

Things had gotten worst. Mama's man who later became her husband started beating her after the last child was born. It eventually affected her health. Mama's man started a couple of odd jobs to bring more income into the house. He would do a variety of jobs including cleaning up, cutting the white man's grass, washing windows, picking pecans and still able to manage a full-time job working for the city. Sometimes we would join him in his work. Mostly my little brother would help him. You would think we were the best dress children in the school, but this was never the case.

Now I always remember feeling good when he was not there. I would secretly hope that he would never come back. He would eventually find his way home. He had mama's mind right where he wanted it to be, locked in her insecurity. If we did anything wrong, she would surely let him know once he came through those doors. She would make her report as he would always find his way back. Long after the sun has gone down, when mama's husband come home he would come with a list of work for us to do no matter what had transpired between them. Mama would even get up early in the morning around five and make biscuits from scratch and make a full course breakfast all the time with an old scarf tied around her head, and that old worn out housecoat fix his lunch and off to work he goes.

My brother was always the one who kept them cars and old truck running. He had taught him how to work on them until he got good enough to work on them vehicles on his own, he also had him doing mostly all the yard work and fixing whatever repairs that were needed around the house sometimes whenever he was in a not such good mood or maybe he felt like we just need to be working, we had to move bricks from one side of the yard and the next day move then back to the other side, this went on until he was ready for it to stop, Michael Jackson had nothing on us.

Now there was early morning or sometime late at night working in the garden or field depends on who was paying him for what whether it would be collard greens, peas, turnip greens or whatever he had planted that we had to pick before going to school early that morning or before going to bed at night. Then there was a time when we had to pick shell peas for the house as well and for others who had paid for those peas or any other food from the garden. There were times when we were told to pick on someone else field and that we would be paid for the picking. We could take that money to buy school clothes, unfortunately, we found out that mama man had been paid our money. This meant there was no school clothes money for us; this was heartbreaking.

Some years passed by and mama's man found a new way to generate income. The house we lived in, became a liquor house. No just any liquor house, but the best and only liquor house on the dirt road.

The weekend would start on Thursday, and if it were a holiday, it would be extended into the weekday. There were always people in and out the house, all times of day and night, there was always the latest songs playing on mama's record player. Songs like Shotgun by Junior Walker and all Stars, Satisfaction by Otis Redding, Heat Wave, You really got a hold on me, Mother-n-Law, Mr. Postman, and Stagger Lee Mustang Sally, Scratch my back and much more, people dancing and drinking all times of the day and night, Them old plywood floors would take a beating sometimes you could see the wood jumping up and down and I would watch to see if that wood would break loose from one of those old nails.

Mama always had some food cooking to serve along with those fifty cent shot glasses of liquor she would pour, white lighting, homebrew, beer, etc. Sometimes people would come just to drink their screwdriver, boons farm or whatever was their choice of wine. I can hear them now; this sure is some good chicken, collards greens, cornbread and potato salad. Some would even come saying the word is out that you are a good cook. I just come to get me some of that good food you are cooking. Mama would fix them a plate of food without charging them one penny.

As I stated before there was always music playing in the house. Mama loved her music. She would make sure that she had all the latest songs. Every year around the holidays, mama had the house filled with Christmas music such as William Bell what do the lonely do at Christmas. The Supremes Holiday, Rudolph the red-nosed reindeer by the Temptation. This Christmas by Donny Hathaway. That old familiar Christmas song by the Temptation White Christmas, or Merry Christmas Baby by Otis Redding I think you get the point, mama loved her music, Christmas was mama's favorite holiday, I believe that it had a way of making her feel happy and sad at the same time.

Hospital and mishaps

Now on this one particular extended holiday weekend, I woke up to music playing, people dancing, loud talking and a big pile of coats thrown on top of me as I lay in my bed. I was hot. Most time I was considered a sickly child because I had asthma. It was always hard for me to breath. It seems as if each breath would be my last breath. Mama always had a watchful eye on me. This particular night I was feeling awful, I had the worst backache I had ever felt. I woke up crying with all those coats on top of me. I was very hot, and the crying and moaning must have scared my sister. She jumped out of that top bunk bed and ran to tell mama that something was wrong with me, all I could do was cry. Mama rushed in to see what was wrong and began to call for her man. He came running and saw that something was terribly wrong. He picked me up in his arms, wrap that old blanket around me and rushes off to the car; mama was at his side. They rushed me to the hospital; perhaps he saw the fear in mama's eyes knowing that she didn't want anything to happen to her baby girl or was it just the Lord looking out for me. I like to believe it was both cases.

I later heard him telling the story at the table with his drinking friends, the Dr. said one moment later, and that child would have died she could have died from pneumonia. Well, I guess I know how to stop a party. Now mama man had a brother who was considered you know how they say; he was a crazy and wild man who walks the streets with a pack of dogs following behind him. They were just good old country guys, who liked to go fishing. One particular day mama and her man decided to go fishing along with his brother. They decided to take us, children, along. I was afraid of the woods and did not think the old Neuse River was a pretty place for anyone to be. It had lots of trees, small ponds all around and the sand was an ugly brown. I tried to watch very carefully where and how I took each step. I decided to take a slightly different way from mama; she must have had me in her view because before she could adequately warn me, I stepped into quicksand and began to go under. Mama's man's brother came out of nowhere and snatched me out of the quicksand; it was as if he was superman. From that day on, I never saw him as an old drunk man but the man who saved my life. God knew that I had to be here this day. God did not want me to die of what would have been a horrible death. It was a beautiful day. It was my sweet sixteen birthday, it was anything but sweet, yet still, it was a good. I remember feeling good about it. I was glad that I was alive to see that day not so much sickness as before. I could breathe, and those asthma attacks were becoming less and less. I was feeling good. As I sit on the back of the old station wagon with the tail down, I put pink hair rollers in my hair; they were my birthday present. As I continued to sit, I felt that old station wagon start to roll and before I knew it I was pinned between that old station wagon and a truck that was parked right behind the station wagon. It rolled until my legs were pin-up pretty good. I must have screamed at the top of my lungs because everyone came out of their houses and those that were outside came running too! What's wrong one said? What's the matter said another, but as soon as my younger brother saw what had happened, he ran inside the house and grabbed the truck keys returned and then he jumped in the truck and backed the truck out of the way so that my legs could be free. It took me few minutes before I regained my composure and was able to walk. After all the excitement had died down, I heard a voice that said the devil wanted to take you out. Well, I didn't understand who exactly was speaking, so I ignored the voice today I know it was the voice of God. There was still another time when my sister and I were over my mama favorite cousin house. She left us at the house while she went to the store. She said she would be right back, well her right back, seemed like a long time to me, so as I was waiting I began pacing around the yard right in front of her brick house. The next thing I knew, I had walked straight into that brick wall and burst a hole right in the middle of my forehead. It was just me and my sister at the house. My sister ran and grabbed that old tin wash pan and told me to hold my head in the was pan so that they blood could run into it. That was a lot of blood. It stopped right before mama's cousin came.

There was a time when mama would send us to next door to the neighbors house to watch out for the school bus, this way mama could keep an eye on us as we waited for the school bus. Well on one particular day, as usual, we went to the neighbor to wait for the bus, as soon as I opened the screen door to the neighbors house, I was attacked by this big wasp nest. Wasp were everywhere. I was running and screaming trying to get away. Mama had to be looking out the kitchen window. The next thing that I knew, she was there trying to see what was wrong. She came like super women out of nowhere running. Wasp were everywhere, mama was trying to fight them off as well. the only thing I remember after that was mama and I coming home from the hospital. We were stung up pretty bad after spending a day in the hospital.

Missing School

In the cold winter season when the boys were still little, mama's man would call me early in the morning and tell me to get in the bed with the babies while mama took him to work. He called me Sandal because he could not pronounce my name correctly due to his stutter. By the time my mama returned home, the school bus was long gone, so it was obvious that I would not be going to school that day.

When I finally returned to school, I was standing around my teacher's desk as she told classmates that they, "passed to the next grade." When she didn't tell me this, I asked her, "did I pass to next grade?" She replied, "oh no baby, I can not pass you to the next grade because you missed over half the school year." Lord, I didn't know that I had missed over half of the school year, tending to mama babies, I had never felt so heartbroken. I loved going to school. I could not understand what was happening in my life.

That year, my self-esteem dropped. I was so embarrassed to see my classmates go on without me. I focused so much on being left behind that I couldn't catch up and low self-esteem set in, deeply within me. My lack of self-esteem brought with it, other demons. That of feeling worthless, hopeless and in eternal despair. I felt that I was only good enough to take care of mama's boys. I could only hope, deep down in my heart that, it would not always be this way. I constantly told myself, IT WILL NOT BE THIS WAY ALWAYS.

Kindergarten with the boys

Those little boys were now old enough to start kindergarten. That did not make me happy still. I continued missing school time because mama and her man made sure that I was with them to take the boys to a kindergarten class. I remember thinking to myself, why am I here? The teacher would look at me as if something was wrong; I felt that she didn't understand my presence in her class with the boys. I would sit in a corner and watch as they would run around the classroom. I felt that the teacher knew that something wasn't quite right yet, she couldn't pinpoint it. She once asked my mama, if I was alright. Then she asked me if I would like some paper and a pencil or to read a book. In my most timid voice, I answered, yes.

The Dirt Road

After getting the paper, pencil and book her attention went back to those little kindergarteners. Now as I look back mama was only following her man's orders. He would say take Sandal with you so she can help you with those boys.

Still not a happy home

Once mama was standing in the kitchen cooking while her man was fussing about something, next thing we knew he had the gun pointed at her. He pulled the trigger, the gun went off and fortunately the bullet landed on the refrigerator door. It barely missed mama. He kept that refrigerator for a long time. Mama said that whenever she opened the refrigerator, it reminded her of how he almost shot here. On another occasion while fussing and cussing, he picked up a pot of hot water and hit her in the head, this landed her in the hospital. I wanted my mama to leave this man. He was mean and habitually violent and cruel. He was beyond controlling and always causing some form of pain and suffering. My mother was very much the opposite. She was gentle and kind. She would do anything to please her man. She showed him through her actions that she was in his corner yet it seemed the more she tried to make him happy and happy home nothing was good enough for him. Mama I'm shouting to the top of my lungs with my inside voice PLEASE JUST LEAVE THIS MAN.

You know they say some women like the bad boys/men. I think it's safe to say mama had just a little bit of that liking in her.

Those little old church ladies

The liquor selling was going good and strong by this time. Mama's man was making good money selling liquor. He made so much money that during a conversation with their room door cracked, I could see lots of money, guns, shotguns and a variety of knives under the mattress. This frightened me, so I quickly ran away from the door. I did not want them to know that I had seen that. That would have surely guaranteed a need to be punished.

Business begin to pick up at a new level. The church ladies and those who were not in agreement, called the sheriff on mama man on a regular basis. When the sheriff would come, the liquor would be hidden. Once my brother was told to go and retrieve the liquor from the big old dresser in

The Dirt Road

the boy's room. Mama man had it hid deep down under a pile of clothes. The boys did not keep a clean room, which seems to work out in mama's man favor. The sheriff never wanted to dig through that dirty clothes. He would stand to watch over the other sheriffs with a smug grin on his face. Their searches were never successful.

Mama's man got a clever idea to build some steps to step into the boy's bedroom. The top of the steps would open and close. This allowed him to sit his jars of white liquor inside. This became his liquor stash. When the sheriff would come, mama's man would beckon us to sit on the steps that he had built. We would sit there, and the sheriff had to walk around us to search the boy's room again. I could tell that they knew something wasn't right, but they could not figure it out. The search was unsuccessful. There was a part of me that wanted to tell the sheriff where the liquor was. But mama's man had such a close eye on me. He knew that if anyone gave him away, it would be me. He would distract the sheriffs by asking questions about their personal lives. He was one of the best con men ever. I wanted the sheriff to catch on to him.

A little later, in the springtime, he decided to stop hiding the liquor in the house. He always had these clever ideas. We had an outdoor house just in you are not familiar with an outdoor house, it was the bathroom outside, so he built a shelf under the outhouse which was right where all your business fell. He told my brother, who was around six years old at the time, to go to the outhouse and get a bottle of liquor. So me, always wanting to know what was going on, I followed my brother as he was telling me what he had to do. You should have seen him as he was squirming with all his heart and might trying to reach for that liquor bottle. As soon as he thought he had a good grip on the bottle, it slipped out of his hand and fell into all that human waste, he ran fast to tell mama's man what happen with the hopes that he would understand, but the response was very much the opposite. Mama's man became so angry that he grab that little boy and found the biggest stick or branch he could find, and he beat that boy so bad he tried to beat the skin off that poor child, he beat him so bad, I wanted to kill him, but all I could do was cry.

That most horrible night

Once mama and her man tried something different. They decided that they would go to the club with another couple. I thought the couple seemed nice and I began to hope that their niceness would rub off on mama's man. He wasn't big on taking mama out anywhere, so mama was happy that she would be going out with her man to have some fun. Around four or five in the morning, my sister, brother and I were awakened by some harsh commands. "Get up get out of that bed, get your damn asses up and go outside and clean that damn blood out of my car!" Rubbing my eyes and still half asleep, I walked outside to the car wondering what was going on. When we got to the car, we found mama in the car, as we open the door to see what the matter was, mama was surrounded

The Dirt Road

by blood, blood was everywhere mama man had cut her so bad as he threw rags at us we began to wipe blood off the car seats and cry at the same time mama was helpless she could not move or do anything, and he still wanted to cuss, fuss and slap her around. I began to hit him with all my might I jumped on his back trying to get him off mama, then he began to turn on me beat me and slap me around. I began to run from the car and down the dirt road. I fell into the ditch, and mama man jumped in that ditch on top of me and began to beat me with all his might, he had beat me so badly I was left in the ditch crying hurt and bruised. As I got myself together to get out of the ditch and walk back to the car to check on mama, my sister and brother were still cleaning up blood. They were still being made to clean up blood with tear stained eyes. Someone at some point in time called the ambulance and mama had gone to the hospital, she stayed for what seemed like a week. I remember the house feeling cold and empty. It was a dark and cold week without mama.

That Most Horrible Night

When mama came home from the hospital, she did say that the police said if he beat on her again then there would be charges. Well, the beating did not stop. The violence continued, he would continue to say very mean and nasty things to her and cuss her out at any given point and time. I think now the beating is taking a toll on mama mental, emotional and physical being, yet she stills held on in and out of the mental facility

Living through pain

I began to have nightmares about that horrific night well into my adult years. I would run as fast as I could because he was always chasing me. Like that night he ran me down in the ditch I would say to myself in my nightmare dream if only I can make it to the city limit line, then I would be free from this-this place. I thought to myself if I run backward I can run faster, and he would not be able to catch me, well I never made it to the city limit line to get away, and I could never run fast backward enough. I found out later in life that God was speaking to me in those nightmare dreams and that He wanted me to run to him and not away from what I was going through in life.

It was tough to remain hopeful when depressed. Everything seemed doomed to fail. However, you can gain control over the situation if you believe that God is greater than your situation. We must lay our problems before God in prayer and believe that God can and will give you victory over the problem. God is still on the throne, and he is still in control.

Now I know that God can reach into the devastating parts of your life. He can reach way down deep into the most hurtful part of your life, and he can call deep unto deep. The enemy had a plan, and his plan was to destroy me because I was already dead. God also had a plan that is why those little old church ladies were assigned to pray over our house. God's plan was much greater God knew that somebody in that house would come out alive and accept him wholeheartedly. He could be the only one who embedded the belief that, things would not always be this way. That was all that I had to hold on to. I didn't know any scriptures because we didn't attend church, but I thank God for placing angels of protection to watch over my life. I always felt that I had to deal with the situation before me and I bless God for giving me the confidence to talk to mama about that night. I told her that I always have nightmares regarding that dreadful and scary night. I could still see the hurt in her eyes. I could see that she didn't want to talk about it or didn't know how to talk about it. I didn't want to press the issue because I knew then that it was hard for mama to talk about and express her feelings. I believed that God was dealing with mama in his way. One day, I heard God say, in your running backward you are running from me, run faster to me.

Well, he still would stay out all night or away from the house two or three days during the week. I loved when he did this because it was a guarantee that mama would be ok. There would be no hitting or hurting, but I could always see the hurt in mama's eyes. To deal with the pain, mama started drinking. She stayed around the house and drank all day. Because of this my sister and I had to take care of the little boys. Mama stopped taking care of the house, and she had little to no interest in cooking or cleaning. She was lonely for her man.

I saw the benefits of him being away, no whippings but even so, her mind was still controlled by him, even in his absence. She wouldn't leave him because she feared death. Despite all of this, the liquor house business was going strong.

Hog killing

On occasion, there were some happy moments. A house filled with people caused mama's man to be entertaining. He would dance, and he was an excellent dancer. He would grab mama by the hand and pull her out to dance. She was a good dancer also. They would tear the dance floor up on some of the old songs. The listed to Walking the dog, 6345789, Baby, I Love you, Lonely Tear drops, You've really got a hold on me, people would be drinking, clapping their hands because they just got one heck of performance and it would put a smile on my face too.

They say he was a jack of all trades. With all his other many jobs he would raise hogs and pigs, and he made good money selling them to the hog market. With all the people he knew, during hog

Hog Killing

killing season there would be a high volume of traffic on that dirt road. All kinds of people would come through. He would have a hog killing party which seemed to last an entire week. He would wake us kids early in the morning because school was out. He would have us to come outside and stand to watch as he grab a knife walk up to that hog he already had hanging upside down on gallops and start from the neck of the hog all the way down, he would cut that hog wide open and blood would run down to the ground we stood frozen to see this horrible sight then he would make us continue to stand and watch as he move to the next hog in the pen. He would pick up his shotgun and say watch this, he would aim his gun straight at that hog forehead and shot him right in the middle of its head and kill that hog fear had me frozen I could not move wondering in my mind, why he would want us to see this horrible sight now everyone who came to the house was looking to benefit from helping out with the killing process of the hogs Everyone had their hand out, they would set up an assembly line

The Dirt Road

to get this meat process under way and mama still finding time to pour those fifty shots of liquor, and oh no we were not excluded from the process, my sister, brother and I had a part to play. There was much excitement all around I think the only thing I hated the most and with a passion there were a million trillion of flies I wondered who was going to eat this meat, with all these flies around and on it someone said when you cook the meat the heat will kill all germs somehow it still didn't set right with me. Well it seem like anywhere they had pigs meat outside inside once they got particular part of the meat they wanted it was cut up into different parts, the women would start cooking pork chops, making lard, skins, chitterlings crackling cornbread, things would come from the garden collards green, peas corn on the cob, butter beans and okra. He was the man he had it going on, and I knew others thought he was the man as well because all who was there got some meat for their home as well as some food from the garden.

Hog Killing

The music was jumping, those fifty cents shots was still being poured the little children was running in and out of the house playing up and down the dirt road riding their bikes the older boys along with other boys who lived on the dirt road enjoyed lifting back ends of cars for recreational fun to see who was the strongest or bench pressing on the dirt road, the dirt road was busy very much alive but you never knew what would happen at any given day or time.

Men would come with their women to buy their shots of liquor. They would be drinking and talking, and in the next breath, an argument or fight would break out. I would see some of the most beautiful ladies come to the house with their men. One lady was so beautiful; she had long black hair that locked into curls, pretty skin and a nice shape. I would ask mama why this lady would be with a man who beat her. Mama would give a soft answer, I do not know, or that is who she wants to be with. They would come back weeks later, and her eyes would be black and blue. The lady didn't look happy but was with her man, sometime later, we learned that the beautiful lady died.

Once at one of the liquor drinking parties this man, started fussing and hitting on his women/wife, not sure which one she was to him. I found it strange that mama man had no problem beating mama, but when he saw another man beat his women, he would quickly run to that woman's defense. So it was ok for him to beat his woman, but he would bring out his gun on another man beating his woman. He would threaten to blow someone's damn head off if they continued. Lord help me to understand what is going on here I am just a child, and even I know this does not make sense.

Not only did beautiful ladies come to the house, but there were also woman who came to the house with men who would pay mama's man for a room. The boy's room would be reserved for this because the boys were at grandma's house. He knew how to make a deal, and his friends would go for it. They were drunk and did not care about anything except for getting what they wanted.

Hog Killing

Mama didn't have friends if anything maybe one or two that she valued as friends. This one friend always came to the house. Mama found out that one of them was sleeping with her man and had given birth to a child. This hurt her. I felt that she had more than enough reasons to leave him, but she did not.

The children mama had before she met him could not see their father because he did not permit it. However, my older sister would spend time with her father. I guess it was because he was a military man and I thinks he was just a little bit afraid of him. I remember once he came to see my sister I guess I must have been looking pitifully because my father was not coming around, so he said to mama I'll take both girls out to have fun, now it only should have been my sister and her father day, but mama agreed that I could go, he was a very nice man he brought me something too well, but my happiness was short lived because mama man raise so much hell about that eventually my sister daddy stop coming around, I guess you can say her happiness was short lived as well.

State Fair

Now with all that hard living and living in fear of mama man, I must be truthful, the Lord would always let a glimmer of sunshine in on us. Every year at the State fair we didn't have to ask or plead and beg mama too hard to go to the fair. Mama had a cousin whom she said was her favorite cousin because she would help mama take care of us girls, she would do things like take us to get our hair fixed at the beauty salon. Sometimes she would help buy us school clothes, but that was on rare occasion. The fair was a big deal to us, it was the only time we got to get off that dirt road for a minute and have some fun, so mama cousin would come and take us into town not sure if mama knew but she would drop us off at the fair or sometimes she would let us catch the city bus to the fair, and we would have the best time, sometimes we would even get to go two or three before the fair left.

By this time those four little boys were growing up. They were coming into their personality doing their own thing. One of those boys my sister and me and I would teach him the latest dance moves, that little boy would catch on so quickly, when paying customer would come to the house they heard how good of a dancer he was, they would say let that little fellow dance for us, he would dance, he would dance his little heart out and put on a great performance, Michael Jackson had nothing on him. That little dude could dance at the end of the dance they would throw money at his feet. I would say boy pick up your money he would put on a show for them. They would always tell mama man that little boy has something special in him. He did not like hearing that because he saw that something different in him but couldn't quite put his finger on it, or he saw it, and it was hard for him to deal with. He was not his favorite child, and my brother could feel that.

The Dirt Road

Now mama man had been married before and had two children from his previous marriage. The children were older than mama older children. They finished school and went off to the military and or college once returning home, the younger one, I heard the grown folks say, was shell shot and that the military had messed his mind up. He was a drill sergeant in the military whenever he would come home on leave there was more drama in the house. We had to deal with him waking up early in the morning doing drills, once we were awakened to the sound of move it, one two three four I said move it then we were made to line up on the wall of our living room with a gun facing us we were told by mama man to do whatever he said because he could pull the trigger at any point in time, as we stood there with a gun pull on us not really knowing what was going on, he was talking then he began to cry then he would take a drink of liquor we just had to stand until the situation calm down not knowing how it would end, but mama man finally got him under control.

State Fair

We were saved that night; the Lord was with us once again. In the process of time as I was walking into the bedroom I saw mama man son tied to the bed post, I was told that the son had gotten so out of control that his daddy couldn't do anything with him, he had to wrestle him down, and hog tied him to the bed.

Once again things had gotten so bad mama man was on the rampage doing his usual fussing and cussing shouting all kind of death threats not only at mama this time but to the whole house. Even to his little boys. Things were so out of control that night that grandpa, his daddy had come down to the house which he only lived a couple of houses away. He came to try to reason with his son, I heard him say boy, please put the gun down, boy this ain't no way to treat your wife and kids, you got these little boys here put the gun down, son, before you hurt someone I hear him say, papa, I'll kill every damn one of them, now this was a first because he was crying as he threaten to kill us. I guess his papa felt he had done all he could do and said all he could say because he was a very calm man, so his papa left, because he could not reason with him so once again I go into my mind and say why would he leave us here at gun point, the little old church ladies had to been praying for us because a few moments later as his papa walk out the door he put the gun down, once again the Lord was on our side.

Disappointed

Mama finally made her mind up to leave him. She had finally had enough of, this type of living, so she called for her cousin to come and get her, we were so happy. We were leaving the dirt road, our knight in shining armor had shown up to rescue us. "Come," she says to mama, "get your children and get in the car whatever you don't have we can get for you later let's go." Yeah oh boy we were so happy you can stay with me until we work things out for you to get you own place ok kids get in the car then we heard those dreadful words, "I CAN'T GO." It felt like my heart stop, and I couldn't breathe. I said to mama, "this man is beating you, mama, why can't you leave why won't you leave?" With tears flowing down our faces, we were so mad at mama we are telling her your cousin is here to take us away from this madman, this mad house and this crazy life mama we don't need him we can make without him we'll help you with the boys we'll get jobs we will do whatever it take to help you please just leave. Please, mama, get in the car we beg mama why won't you leave?" Then mama gives up her big reason why she can't leave. Mama said she was afraid to leave because he said he would find her and take those four boys and kill her in the process, mama we will call the police if he comes, her cousin says, "I can't leave you here, you know I am here for you, why won't you come? You can stay with me until you get yourself together." "Thanks," said mama, "but I better stay." Mama, cousin, left very disappointed, she left without us, as I saw that car drive away up and out of that dirt road I was so hurt and mad at mama, my sister and I went around the back of the house crying as if someone had stabbed us in the heart, and we said some pretty mean things about our mama, she can leave our daddies but she can't leave this man who is beating her brains out,

Disappointed

Mama finally made her mind up to leave him. She had finally had enough of, this type of living, so she called for her cousin to come and get her, we were so happy. We were leaving the dirt road, our knight in shining armor had shown up to rescue us. "Come," she says to mama, "get your children and get in the car whatever you don't have we can get for you later let's go." Yeah oh boy we were so happy you can stay with me until we work things out for you to get you own place ok kids get in the car then we heard those dreadful words, "I CAN'T GO." It felt like my heart stop, and I couldn't breathe. I said to mama, "this man is beating you, mama, why can't you leave why won't you leave?" With tears flowing down our faces, we were so mad at mama we are telling her your

The Dirt Road

cousin is here to take us away from this madman, this mad house and this crazy life mama we don't need him we can make without him we'll help you with the boys we'll get jobs we will do whatever it take to help you please just leave. Please, mama, get in the car we beg mama why won't you leave?" Then mama gives up her big reason why she can't leave. Mama said she was afraid to leave because he said he would find her and take those four boys and kill her in the process, mama we will call the police if he comes, her cousin says, "I can't leave you here, you know I am here for you, why won't you come? You can stay with me until you get yourself together." "Thanks," said mama, "but I better stay." Mama, cousin, left very disappointed, she left without us, as I saw that car drive away up and out of that dirt road I was so hurt and mad at mama, my sister and I went around the back of the house crying as if someone had stabbed us in the heart, and we said some pretty mean things about our mama, she can leave our daddies but she can't leave this man who is beating her brains out,

Disappointed

they say my daddy is a good man, Lord help me to understand, Lord what is wrong with mama? I would sit around days after trying to come up with a plan and plot to kill this man; then we would be free from him. Maybe a little rat poison in his food or a little Clorox in his liquor, oh but the fear of God had a grip on my life, and the thought of prison stopped that thinking, Lord why are we here in this terrible situation? Lord, what did we do that was so wrong that caused us to be here? I can't understand it and Lord I want to be so mad at you, but my heart just won't let me be, why can't I be mad at you Lord? I know you know what is going on here Lord, I have such a deep feeling of hatred for this man, please kill him, I am just a child, am I supposed to know hate like this? Why are you not stopping this? Do you even care about us? Why is this man so mean to mama and her three children who are not his? What are we going to do Lord if I can't kill him then you can you please do it, Lord, we need your help! I just want him dead and out of our lives forever. God was silent. Well, we were back to our normal routine feeling and emotions still messed up because the Lord had not delivered us because God has not answered my prayer I decided that this is just the way life is supposed to be.

Mama still got up before dawn, drunk or sober and made those homemade biscuits and cooked breakfast and saw her man off to work and got us kids off to school whenever we did not have to stay home life was interesting. I liked school; it was a safe place for me. I felt free and untouchable I had good friends who didn't know what my household was like.

Once that little different son of his who he called, different, every chance he got they really didn't bond that well like his other sons he could not understand why he was so much of a different child, once that child was outside playing and was throwing some rocks as little boys do, a rock hit the car window and shattered that window, he beat that little boy so bad I thought he was going to beat him to death he beat him so bad, I cried as if he was beating me too, mama would always turn a deaf ear whenever he was beating any of her children, she did this because it was in the best interest of everyone, because if she tried to stop the beating she would get a beating too.

So as I lay here in this top bunk bed, I hear mama crying and pleading for him to stop hitting her, Lord where are you? I can't see nor can I hear you I know you see what's going on here, why are you letting this happen? Do something, you are God, why don't you stop this but somehow I do sense your presence, he gave me peace and calmness soon her crying stop.

Traveling time

Mama's grandma, whom we called mother, on the Georgia side would come to visit us because mama had stopped going to see her people. Mother would plead with mama to stop living with this man. She would often tell mama to return home to receive her inheritance. Each time, mother would leave with a disappointed look on her face. Mama thought that mother was always trying to run her life and tell her how to live. I would over hear mama say that mother was getting on her nerves. Mama would not allow anyone, and I do mean, anyone to talk about her man. She had no intentions of letting anyone come between them, no matter how frequently he broke her heart. Mama loved her man. When he was not home, she would protect that house like she was a watch dog.

She would not let anyone bother anything that belonged to him in or outside of the house. If you came up in the yard and thought that you were going to get something that belonged to him, you may as well think again. It didn't matter who you were; she did not discriminate.

On a couple of occasions, we went to see mama's man son. He lived a couple of hours away. He wasn't big on traveling, especially with mama and us children. When we arrived, the party ensued. Drinking, music and loud conversation continued. He found out that his son was beating his wife and holding her at gunpoint. I couldn't understand how he would tell someone else to stop beating their wife. An argument broke out as a result of this conversation, and the son did not hesitate to remind his dad, whose house he was in.

One time we went to visit his sister who lived in Philly, as we entered the city, he got lost and asked directions of a man who was standing on the corner. The man told him that he didn't know and I guess he thought he was the big man there, so he responded to the man saying, "what do you mean, you don't know, you live around here." The man responded, "yeah, I live around here, but you are the one who is lost not me." I know that I should not have been laughing, but I was happy that someone who wasn't afraid of him put him in his place.

I guess mama thought that because he was in a traveling mood, she would ask him to take her home to Georgia to see her people. Somehow he agreed to take the whole family. Mama was so excited to be going! She told us to pack our bags because we would be leaving as soon as he got off. We too were excited. The happiness was short lived because we waited and waited and then night fall came, and there was no sign of her man. Somehow mama got word that he had gone to New Jersey with some friends and stayed a few days. While there he met a woman who took him for every penny he had. He returned home with his head tucked between his tail. The woman must have done a number on him because he showed a little bit of humility. He was nicer to mama, and she took care of him.

Even though she was hurt, you could see the hurt in her eyes she put on her best show to hold it together, he held in his anger for a few days because guilt and shame had a hold on him, then it wasn't long he was back to his old self.

Now believe it or not there are some life lessons you can learn growing up in a liquor house one how a lady should not act. There were these drunk ladies who came, and they were drunk out of their minds. I don't think one of the ladies had a clue that she was sitting with her legs so wide open that you saw all God gave her. It was revealing to everyone in the room, oh my God those little boys picked on her so bad. My sister and I picked on the other lady that was with her she was telling here to close her legs. The lady was so drunk out of her mind until she just slid right out of the chair onto the floor. I remember saying to myself, that is what I don't want to be like. Now some long years later I was in church, and I see this familiar face, and it brings me back to my childhood, I suddenly remember this lady who used to come to the dirt road liquor house, now she sits in church. After church I went to ask her if she knew my mama man, her answer was yes I know him. We would come to your house, y'all was just little children back then, I didn't let on that I knew her secret because I had seen the beautiful work God had done. She had expressed to me that God had done a new thing in her life. I was glad for her, not only was he doing a new thing in her life, in my life as well. He was letting me know that things and situation could and would change. God had a plan that I didn't quite understand. God has a divine purpose for everything that happens in our life. He wants to use this situation to bring about his perfect will in our life.

Then there was mama's man favorite cousin who came on a regular; he was a big man, clothes always dirty and smelling. He always had a big glob of snuff or chewing tobacco packed in the corner of his mouth. I never saw him remove that snuff or tobacco for anything, not even to eat or drink, and he sure did love mama cooking and those fifty cents shots she would pour. Then one day something amazing happened that had me in awe, he came all clean up, had taken a bath and that big glob of snuff or tobacco was gone. He was dressed in a suit and a tie. He had come to tell his favorite cousin mama's man, that he had received the Lord in his life and that he had started going to church and he was inviting him to accept the Lord into his life. Well mama' man pick on his cousin so bad, until he took again another one of mama fifty cents shot only this time his cousin poured it for him, he did his usual thing, he took that drink only this time all dressed up. A couple of weeks or so went by; mama man favorite cousin came again still wearing suit and tie but the big glob still removed from the corner of his mouth. Again he asked his cousin to receive the Lord in his life and to informed him that he had started a small church and was preaching the word of God. Just like before mama man picked on his cousin a second time, only this time the man would leave without taking one of mama famous fifty cents shots. The word was he preach the word of God in his little small church in the back of his house until he pass away, it was so amazing to me because I had never seen something so defile and disgusting change into something so complete opposite what a transformation.

There were times when my sister and I were allowed to spend the weekend with mama aunt. She was such a sweet little frame of a lady who loved the Lord. Whenever we went to her house, we totally changed, she would make little ladies out of us dress us in lace and ruffles. She would make us recite poems or Bible verses, and she taught us how to bow and curtsey. She said this is how little girls are supposed to act. She taught us all the things a girl should know, how to fold a handkerchief, how a little girl is expected to sit, how we should protect ourselves whenever we are walking the street alone going to the store, she said to make sure you keep your money real close to you. She would give us a dime for a telephone call along with our quarter it needed to be tied up in a handkerchief and safety pin close to our clothes. Mama loved her aunt, I think she must have gotten to mama about the things and ways of girls are to be, mama start letting us go to that church them little old ladies say that they would make sure we were taken care of, we got in the children's choir and attended vacation bible school in the summer, sometimes we even went to Sunday school. Mama auntie was right there when we got baptized in that old dirty, muddy pond; she stood there looking as proud as can be as we got out of the water waiting to be wrap in an old white sheet. I think mama was happy that day knowing that she had allowed something good to happen, mama auntie went home well pleased.

I asked about what we were to do now that we were baptized. Everyone looked at me with that puzzled look on their face. After a moment of silence, one of the girls that had gotten baptize along with us spoke up and said that we should party, so we put on some records on mama records player and dance the whole evening away. There was this feeling inside of me that this was not the right thing to do, since mama didn't know and her auntie was long gone home, so we did what was normal for us DANCE, it was our way of celebrating this special day.

It wasn't long before, and mama man was back to their usual routine. Being mean and still ruling over us with an iron fist. The little boys were growing up and coming into their personalities. The older children were growing up as well. We still had to do whatever was told to us. We wanted to be involved with games and activities at school, but mama always directed us to ask her man. It sometimes took us days and weeks to build up enough courage to ask him anything. Our requests were always met with a disappointing, no. We were always reminded that if we did anything wrong, we would get that drop cord that was waiting for us tied around that old door handle. We could it see every time we walk pass it. Once when he was in a good mood he allowed one of our friends to come over we were in the back bedroom laughing and talking doing hair as girls do, so we decide to cut our hair, we were now taking care of our hair anyway, at this point because mama didn't fool with it that much anymore, mama noticed what we had done and said to her man, those girls have cut their hair, he called us into the living room and saw what we had done, then was told to go back to our room, he came in that room with that drop cord and beat us so bad with our friend still in there with us, she did her best to console after the beating we were so mad hurt and upset with our mama because we could not understand why she would tell him anything about our hair, since she was not taking care of it any more, once I was sitting watching tv he said something I didn't give the right answer, or he was just plain mad as usual maybe not sure he pick up one of his old steel toe boots and hit me in the head with it but I blocked the hit with my hand, I ended up with a broken finger.

I always wondered why I was placed in this situation. I would ask God why He hated me so much to put me in place like this. I had only a childlike understanding. It was truly hard to understand what was going on in my life. Our household was so much different than others. I remember deciding, Lord one of these old days when I get out of here, I am going to tell the story of what the dirt road was really like, now when we had gotten older, and we would be standing around reminiscing on some of the past events that went down on the dirt road, someone would say if only this path could talk there would be a lot of stories to tell I would always say, it can talk I am going to tell it but wait for the book, we would laugh and continue our reminiscing. Some would say those was the good old days and some would say those was the worst of days.

I think one of the best days I had with mama man was when he took me with him to sell the pigs that he raised to the hog market. For some reason he was nice that day the hog market was the last place I wanted to be and I didn't have any say so about that it was a scorching day and a very smelly place to be, but at least he was nice and very peaceful that day he gave me money to buy whatever I wanted, I could only think, maybe he getting better, the Lord had let the sunshine that day and he actually treated me like I was a human being, sometime God will give peace in the middle of our storm.

Now there were times when mama man would give us life lessons, advice and speeches. He would say things like, whatever you planning on being in life, be your best at it, I don't care if you become a whore, be the best damn whore around, another one of his sayings didn't be anybody flucking fool, I don't care who they are family friend or foe, people will use and abuse until there is nothing left of you, another thing he would say, if you don't put anything into the system don't expect to get anything out of the system, because he would work from the sun up to the sun down. He knew he was making his contribution to the system and he had something to fall on when he retired, and his most famous saying was, people can't help the way they are, if you born crazy you gonna die crazy as if he believe that people could not change at all. This became his famous saying that everyone was saying it because it was always said at every one of his closing speeches, even the grandchildren and the great-grandchildren knew this famous saying, "If you born crazy you gonna die crazy."

The dirt road eventually expanded and became city controlled. We lived about a half mile from the city, so the city incorporated the dirt road. This also meant that we now lived in the city. This change interfered with raising pigs. The state agriculture wanted mama's man to stop feeding the pigs table scraps and begin using hog feed. He ranted and raved and had all types of fits about his. He was not happy and thought about how it would impact his income. He tried it for a while and then stopped. He still had other ways to make up for that income. He was a jack of all trades. He knew how to get free labor out of people. Because he was good at making money, people would always come to him needing something to ride. He always had one or two old cars in the back yard he would let someone borrow, but they had to pay him for it. It was nothing for someone to borrow money. He would always make sure that he got his money back. He always had what people needed or wanted. No one got away with not paying him back. Oh, the man had many skills not only did he rule over our lives, but those who was not as well off as he was. He could command and demand anything of anyone, especially if he knew they were weak enough to do what he said and it was nothing for him to cash someone small check, he would give them the cash, and they were happy, some people look up to him.

Now here I am again trying to understand, Lord help me I am not liking the things I am seeing. Whenever he had to deal with the white man, it was yes sir or boss. He was always on his best behavior. I was conflicted by his identity. I could not understand why he was so good away from home. He terrorized our house, but in the community, he was deemed a hero. He even received a humanitarian award for saving a man's life. Lord, I did not understand this picture. He had dual personalities.

The Dirt Road

Mama has been beaten into bad health now she was constantly checking in and out of the Mental health facilities. Leaving was never on her mind. The boys were getting older, and by this time her older children had left home. We continued to worry about mama being there with him. I went home frequently to check on her. I was older and waited for him to lay a hand on her. He was a smart man and he knew not to try that in my presence. Mama shared that he had risen to strike her during one of his angry moods and the oldest son, who was still living at home, saw what was happening and told his dad, that if he laid a hand on her, he would kill him. I was so happy to hear this and to know that he had the courage to step up to him. After this, he never hit mama again, but the fussing and cussing ceased.

While at work one day, mama called me. She never called us at work unless it was very important. Apparently, her man fell out at work and was now laying in the ICU unconscious. He was unconscious for two or three days. Mama stayed by his side during this time, and she did not leave the hospital until he left.

Somewhere during that time after coming home from his comatose state, the beating finally did stop thank you, Lord. Mama had some difficult situation to deal with; I earnestly believe that she had placed them all in the hands of the Lord. When you are sensitive to the Holy Spirit, he will transform your despair into hope and your depression into a celebration.

Now the liquor house was slowly coming to a cease; the new generation began smoking weed. Mama's man was not allowing that stuff in his house because he did not smoke weed. So this caused a decline in his business. Guess what? Mama man started going to church. I believe those little old church ladies prayers had been answered because some of them had been called home to be with the Lord they put down some prayer before they left here.

I often wondered why his mama, who was a devout Christian, had such a bad child. She would go to church every Sunday. She saw her son raise hell, beat his wife and rule over the house. Yet, she could not say one word to change his heart. She would always say that her son was good. I was so confused, who was this good son that she was referring to? I now think it was her faith talking. His mother read her Bible every Saturday and Sunday school lesson without fail. As I would go, sometimes, she would always share words of encouragement. She would say that I was a sweet child because I took the time to sit with older people. I knew that she was praying for our household and her son. There wasn't anything that her son wouldn't do for her. He took excellent care of her. The Holy Spirit later revealed that it was her prayers that were holding the dirt road together.

God was giving all of us a chance to get our lives right. He allowed the sun to shine on the dirt road continually, even with all of the wrongdoing that was going on there. God had mercy on us, and through her prayers, we had a chance to get right with him. She was the seed that the Lord placed there, and it took all of forty years for most of us to get right. When grandma died, the Lord lifted his spirit from the dirt road, and you could see that his presence was no longer there.

Long before mama's man's mama died, he started attending church. God had a plan for mama, and it did not lie dormant because God was still at work. God says his word does not return to him void, even when we don't understand, the plan of God does not mean he does not know he made the plan, so he very well understands we just have to walk it out and trust God that he knows what he is doing. Well as a child I had no idea what God was doing, I only know what I saw and what I saw I could not see God in it because I was always looking for the natural. Maybe I saw God but ignored him. One thing I do know is that I could feel his presence which allowed me to trust him. I kept saying that, things will not always be this way and that they would get better. I always had a strong desire to go to church, even though I was not brought up in the church. I believed that not only would things get better, but they would also get better for mama as well. I didn't have to pray for them to get better, I thanked him for them getting better. I had strong faith that they would do just that, get better.

When mama's man's papa died, it was a sad day. He was the nicest and calmest man that I ever met as a child. I could not understand how such a quiet and meek person could have bore a child who was so opposite. When His mama died, she was 100. I came home to see my mama, and as I walked into the house, mama's man was crying. I had never seen him cry before. Only this time it was a different type of cry; it was much deeper. I asked him what was wrong, and reached out to touch him gently on the back, and he began to cry even more and he said that he missed his mama. I tried to console him by saying that he would be ok and that his mama was in a better place. He said something nice to me, and that word was ok. It was the first touching moment that we ever had. I didn't know how to react. I felt sad because he was sad. This was the first real feeling that I ever had for him. Lord, I didn't think I was supposed to be feeling that way. I wanted to hate him, but I couldn't find the ability to hate him. But something was happening to me in my soul.

The spirit of compassion has come over me Lord your spirit has taken over, so I yield now for the first time, I have to reach out and show some love to this man, this is hard because my heart still don't want to and really don't know how, but I did it, God plan was not just for him it was for me too, because I really hated this man who was not loving to mama or to me, God can remove that heart of stone, how great is our God who can do the unimaginable the unthinkable.

My visit was cut short because I was so filled. When I left, all I could do was cry during my drive home. I felt some comfort leaving mama there with him. Things seemed to be slowly changing for the better. Mama seemed a little happier. How great is my God, things were getting better. So much so that on some occasions, I would visit mama and she would be doing her nails or a puzzle book. Her man had brought her some new shoes, a pocketbook or a dress. He was doing things that he had never done before. He had stopped cussing and fussing and began to treat her like his wife.

Now by this time, mama had completely stopped all cooking because of her health, so guess who was doing all cooking? Her man and he was taking care of the household chores. He was taking care of mama and making sure she was at her Dr's appointments. They would even go places together like visiting other couples and family members. Mama was now getting what she had always longed for. We often go home because the dirt road is home. Someone is always coming and going.

The young generation changed the name of the dirt road to the path. They brought new demons which included smoking weed. People would come and go to buy and smoke weed. Mama's man did not allow this in his house. People would state that he must have forgotten that he use to run a liquor house. At any rate, they respected him. They also knew that he was getting up in age and the thieves would steal anything nailed down from him to get drug money. The dirt road was infected in a new way.

There would be what they called, drug parties, people from everywhere would come to the path blasting music.

There is another scripture that speaks volume to me. I learn this scripture as a young adult. James 1:1-4 *"Dear brothers, is your life full of difficulties and temptations? Then be happy. For when the way is rough your patience has a chance to grow. So let it grows, and don't try to squirm out of your problems. For when your patience is finally in full bloom, then you will be ready for anything, strong in character, full and complete."*

Don't you love how God can take what we feel is the worse situation in our lives and use them to grow us up? When you feel that He has forgotten or you can not see your way out, He is present. God knows how to build character to make you secure and complete. When I thought the best thing for us to do was to leave mama just leave this crazy man. I am so glad that God had a plan different from mine. As I often think back on that night, if mama had left, then we would have been living in the city and there was no telling what was waiting on us there. Things really could have been worse than they were. We could have ended up in foster care, jail or sold out to the streets. Trust God; He always knows what He is doing. He always knows what is best. Sometimes we must go through the valley (dirt road) to reach the mountaintop. As I looked back, I see the dirt road as a safety place.

Lamentations 3:22-24 *"yet there is one ray of hope: his compassion never ends. It is the Lord's mercies that have kept us from complete destruction. Great is his faithfulness; his loving-kindness begins each day afresh. My soul claims the Lord as my inheritance; therefore I will hope in him."* As I said earlier, I didn't know the Lord as a child. All I knew is that it would not be this way always, that's where my hope was. I knew I had to trust in something. I believe that is what God gave me to trust in and to stand firmly on.

I can not say that I believed that trouble was temporary or that it didn't last always. God gave me His word in a way that I could understand. He knew that I didn't have scripture to stand on. Sometimes in life, we have to grab onto whatever seems reasonable and right because God's word says, he has given us a fair amount of faith. He will continue to build on that faith. This was my reasonable amount of faith; it want be this way always. I tell you somewhere, and somehow, you are going to reach back in your past and deal with hurt and pain that someone else may have created for you but have left it undone for you to deal with.

Build up, I say build up, there is a giant in you who is waiting to break down walls and the barriers of low self-esteem, feelings of worthlessness, loneliness, and insecurity. The giant in you will help you to rise and live out your full potential. Only when you are made aware that there are some things in your past that must be dealt with, then you will break free of those things, even if someone else created your pain and unhappiness.

Never underestimate the power that was given to you or who you are. It is critical to have faith in God it is also equally important to have faith in what He gave you and that is faith. You cannot wait until your problems are over to start having faith. Don't wait until the battle is over to shout, I say shout while the fight is still going on, shout now with your battle cry. He can take the seemingly hopeless situation whether it's a family matter, business, bank account and turn it into something great. You lack nothing. God is a multiplier. He can turn that thing into something beyond your wildest expectations.

I was not aware that I was being used by God in my life situation. It was only a test to see how I would handle it. Would I buckle, turn to drugs, run away or allow the problems to overtake my mental state. God kept me in a quiet and secure place in the midst of my entire struggle. My perfect get away was in him, and today God gets all the glory. Some ask, how could you have gone through all that without losing your mind? Although I sometimes looked for love in all the wrong places, I knew that my help came from God. He helped me to become the overcomer that I am today. You too, need to become an overcomer. There is greatness in you. You may be in a place of despair right now, but tap into your greatness. Everytime that the enemy throws things at you while you are down, use those things as building blocks and stand on them. You will reach the top of your situation and will be able to see your way clear. Yes, it will require some work, resilience, and determination but you can do it.

I worked hard to reach my greatness. Sometimes it was so overwhelming until I didn't want to try, but I just could not give up. My mind could not avoid the things I needed to do. I knew I wanted better. I also knew that there had to be better today. I still want better for my life and the life of my children and grandchildren. This pushed me so hard to go back to school and get my high school diploma. I also wanted to improve my job skills. I took a vocational training course at the local Institute and receive a certificate. Later I received an Associate's degree in Biblical Studies. I guess it's like Iyanla says, you have to do the work, so I did the work. It was like mama man said, if you don't put anything in don't expect to get anything out, I guess he was teaching me a life lesson in the only way he knew how and when you think about it does make sense.

I am told that you can learn from anybody, they do not have to be super educated. God can use whomever to speak, if He can speak through a donkey, surely he can speak through mama's man. I am reminded of an occasion while visiting my sister in New York. We went to ride the ferry to Staten Island. It started raining very hard, and my feet became soaked through my tennis shoes. We rushed into the bathroom to dry off, a homeless lady approach me with a paper towel in her hand she gave them to me and told me to take excellent care of my feet, she then said feet are important they need to take you through life. I thought a homeless person is giving me advice well indeed I took her advice and those paper towel too and dried my feet off. God will position people in your life to give you what you need and when you need it. I do know that God will give you the desires of your heart, he will allow us to have the things we want the most even though it may not be right for us, mama loved her man, and I was a part of that package deal, and God allow it because that what she wanted.

I don't know why I always kept score or tried to understand the complexity of the situations. I was told by my older brother, that I was in a bad place at the wrong time, due to no fault of my own. Today I believe that is someone hurts you; you don't spend the rest of your life, keeping score. I found out that I was only hurting myself by holding on to all those bad things. When we walk in God's love, we find freedom by keeping no account of the wrong that was done to us. If you are hurting from the pain of forgiveness ask God to help you to stop keeping score so you can let go of your bitterness.

To bring your up to speed, what was once a dirt road, filled with life, laughter and all kinds of action is now lifeless. The old brick house that I grew up in is just there. Weeds and trees have overgrown the road, and you can barely see the house.

The Dirt Road

No more cars go in or out of that old road. You see, when our beacon of light died, our grandma and those little old church ladies, who kept the road covered in prayer, were all gone. I believed that God placed them there for my good, to keep me protected in prayer from the enemy whose goals was to destroy me.

Two years after the Lord called grandma to her heavenly home, it was then every two years someone else would pass away. Mama man passed away some years later, 2008, and oh yes I forgot to tell you, I along with my older sister and the little brother that was under me we had to call him big daddy under the direction of mama. Lord only knows why she wanted us to call him that, he was a short man who stood the around 5feet 7inches. I would hate to call him that whenever I had to ask or say something to him, I would say it under my breath because I could not find any good about him to call him that.

I never let mama know how much I hated calling him that. I am sure that she could tell by the way I said it. She had chosen that name for me to call him. Some years later, it didn't bother me as much to call him big daddy, probably because I was grown and that was all that I knew to call him. Holding on does more damage than letting go, so I learned to let go of my past hurts and pain and let God. God was working something out in me, and he wanted me to be the best person I could be. He wanted me to have love and compassion even when I did not feel like loving mama's man and believe me there was a time when I did not feel any love for him, as I mentioned before all I had was pure hate for this man but GOD. God knows what it takes for our hearts to pump love. It was my intention to hate mama man until his or mine dying days. I always prayed Lord, please let mama see some happy days before she leave this earth, and God did just that. There were years before mama passed that he had to take care of her, cook for her, wash her cloth, and take mama to and from her doctor's appointment. It gave me pure delight to see him doing those things for my mama. I wish that he could have done that kind of stuff while she was in good health but yet it humble him because now he would take mama on Sunday drives with him after they attended church. He would take her shopping and buy her things. Whenever I would go to see her, mama would say look what he brought me. It seemed as if he was always buying her something to make her happy. They even visited mama's sister for a week, and she shared that he did the right thing. Her face would light up with that smile, and now I could see her happiness coming back.

Mama loved her man. All she wanted from him was his love and kindness. God has a way; He knows how to take something ugly and make it beautiful. I did not hate him so much after he began treating mama well. It looked like he was remorseful for all the wrong things that he had done. Mama stayed there all of those years, dealing with the abuse and it finally appeared as if her faithfulness was paying off, but her body had suffered the consequences. It reminds you of Jesus. He suffered abuse, and he did nothing wrong. Even as I write this letter, I hear God saying that was His way of using her and yes He made it better in the end, because she did find happiness before she passed. I know one of the things she wanted most was for him to put her in a better home. Well, he never did do that so when he passed, God gave mama a much better place to stay. I told mama, I know you wished that you and big daddy could have lived here together and she agreed.

I always thought that I was my mama's favourite child because we often had conversations that allowed me the opportunity to ask her all kinds of questions. Mostly about family including her mom and dad. My siblings didn't ask these questions. I felt that this is what made our bond so strong and special. That's my story, and I am sticking to it. I am certain that my siblings have their different story, I know that she loved us all in her way, because we were different in our own way.

Whatever situation you find yourself in, no matter how dismal your future may seem or how big your problems in life appear, always remember that God is with you and in control of your life. Trust in Him, and He will give you the victory.

I know when I got the victory in my life. It was when I accepted the Lord wholeheartedly. As they say, for real this time, no more going down a dry devil and coming up a wet devil. This was when I purposed in my heart and mind to be sold out for Christ and to live a Christ-like life.

Psalms 23:3 He restored my soul. He guides me in the paths of righteousness for his name sake. Yes, God will lead you through a path (dirt road) so that he may get the glory. As I look back and think of those things, I now know that God had a plan for my life all along. Jesus led me into a glorious future and made me more than a conqueror.

-end-

www.ingramcontent.com/pod-product-compliance
Ingram Content Group UK Ltd.
Pitfield, Milton Keynes, MK11 3LW, UK
UKHW022209230426
12048UKWH00016BA/731